Homemade
MONEY

Twenty-five Realistic Home-Based Businesses

to Build Income, Reduce Dependence,

and Take Control of Your Finances

Bob Wright

Start From Home With Little

Or No Upfront Capital

Learn how to earn your first dollar quickly and grow steadily with practical systems. This book gives you a clear path to building income and control.

Table Of Contents

The Courage to Begin

At some point, almost everyone has imagined it — owning a business of their own.

Not just earning money, but building something. Making decisions without asking permission. Creating income through effort instead of waiting for approval. For some, that idea feels exciting. For others, it feels distant — something reserved for people with more capital, more connections, more confidence.

But the desire is common.

The desire to build.
The desire to control your direction.
The desire to see your effort translate directly into results.

Starting a business is not only a financial decision. It is an act of courage. It means stepping away from complete dependence and accepting responsibility for your own results. It means trusting that small, disciplined actions can grow into something meaningful over time.

Many people delay starting a business because they believe they need significant savings, outside funding, or perfect conditions. In reality, many successful ventures begin with limited resources. Starting with little or no money forces clarity. It encourages careful decision-making, practical action, and disciplined growth. The ideas in this book are built around that principle — begin where you are, use what you have, and grow through structure rather than large financial risk.

This book was written to make that first step practical.

Inside these pages are ideas — real, workable ideas — designed to help you begin. Some are simple. Some require patience. All are structured to be accessible from where you are right now.

You do not need perfect timing.
You do not need extraordinary talent.
You need a starting point.

What follows is not theory. It is a collection of opportunities and systems designed to help you move from intention to action.

And that is where every business begins.

Most people don't hate work.
They hate dependence.

They hate knowing their income depends on one employer, one paycheck, one decision they don't control. When income is fragile, stress rises. When stress rises, options shrink.

Home-based income doesn't remove effort.
It removes helplessness.
It shifts control.

This book isn't about fast money.
It's about building small, controllable income streams from where you already live.

You don't need perfect timing.
You don't need a large investment.
You need structure and disciplined action.

Many people say they want financial freedom. What they truly want is flexibility — the ability to handle emergencies without panic, make decisions without fear, and create income without asking for permission.

That kind of stability isn't built overnight.
It's built gradually.

Not with one idea.
Not in one week.
But through repetition, refinement, and reinvestment.

Inside this book, you'll learn:

- How to choose from 37 practical home-based business models
- How to build a profitable eBay income step by step
- How to test ideas without quitting too soon
- How to develop multiple income streams instead of relying on one

Most people fail not because opportunity is missing, but because their effort is scattered. They jump from idea to idea. They chase excitement instead of systems. They quit before momentum builds.

This book removes the randomness.
It gives you structure.
It gives you a framework.
It gives you options.

You may begin with one income stream. With discipline, it strengthens. With reinvestment, it grows. Over time, small consistent actions compound into measurable progress.

You are not just learning how to make money. You are learning how to build control.

Start small.
Stay consistent.
Track your numbers.
Reinvest wisely.

When you control the source — even partially — confidence replaces anxiety.

And confidence changes everything.

Let's begin.

STARTING SIMPLE

Structure, Taxes, and Common Sense

Before we discuss specific businesses, let's address something that often stops people before they begin.

Legal structure.
Taxes.
Bank accounts.
Licenses.

These topics feel complicated. They don't need to be.

Most small businesses begin as sole proprietorships.

That simply means you are operating as yourself. You provide a service or sell a product. Customers pay you. You track income and expenses. At tax time, that income is reported along with your personal return.

There is no requirement to form an LLC before earning your first dollar. There is no need to build complex systems before you have revenue. Many successful businesses begin with simple structure and evolve over time.

That said, simplicity does not mean carelessness.

Here is a practical starting framework many small businesses follow:

Separate your money early.

As soon as income becomes consistent, open a separate bank account for business activity. This creates clarity and prevents confusion later.

Track income and expenses.

You do not need complex accounting software at the beginning. A simple spreadsheet recording money in and money out is enough. Clarity matters more than complexity.

Understand taxes without panicking.

Business income is generally taxable. Setting aside a percentage of profit for future tax obligations is wise. Many small business owners reserve 20–30% of net profit until they understand their specific situation.

Check local requirements when scaling.

Some services require permits or licenses depending on location. This varies by state and municipality. As income grows and operations become steady, review local regulations and comply accordingly.

Formal structure comes later.

LLCs, expanded systems, and insurance make sense when revenue becomes meaningful. They are growth tools — not starting requirements.

This book does not provide legal or tax advice. Laws vary by state and country. Before making structural decisions, consult a qualified professional in your area.

But do not let complexity prevent action.

Most businesses begin small.
Most start simply.
Structure expands as revenue grows.

Your first goal is not perfection.

It is motion.

CHAPTER 1

Handyman Services

What This Business Really Is

A handyman business is not a construction company. It is a practical problem-solving service for small household repairs and improvements. Most home-owners do not need major remodeling. They need doors repaired, fixtures installed, drywall patched, and small problems handled quickly.

This business is built on reliability, responsiveness, and competence — not perfection.

If you can use basic tools, follow instructions, and show up on time, you can begin.

Why It Works

Every neighborhood has:

Busy homeowners
Elderly residents

Rental property owners
People who delay small repairs

Small jobs are often too minor for contractors but too difficult or time-consuming for homeowners.

That gap is opportunity.

How to Make Your First Dollar

Do not overcomplicate this.

Choose five simple services you can confidently perform:
Replace light fixtures
Install shelves
Repair leaky faucets
Patch drywall
Install curtain rods

Post in three local community groups:

"Local handyman available for small home repairs. Reliable, affordable, and prompt. Message me directly."

Text ten people you know and ask if they need small jobs done.

Offer a flat starter rate for your first few jobs to build momentum.

Your goal is not branding.

Your goal is your first paid job.

The First 30 Days

Focus only on:

Completing small jobs
Getting paid
Asking for referrals
Collecting three to five testimonials

Do not build a website yet.
Do not design a logo.
Do not form an LLC.

Make money first.

Track income and expenses in a simple spreadsheet.

Supplemental vs Full-Time Path

Supplemental Income Model
Five to ten jobs per week
Evening or weekend work
Possible income: $500–$2,000 per month depending
on pricing and effort

Full-Time Model
Twenty-five to forty billable hours per week
Raise rates gradually
Build relationships with property managers
Possible income: $4,000–$8,000+ per month
depending on region

Growth comes from consistency and reputation.

When to Handle Legal and Structure

You can begin as a sole proprietor.

As income becomes steady:

Open a separate business bank account
Track expenses carefully
Review local licensing requirements
Consider general liability insurance

Requirements vary by location. Always verify local
regulations before expanding services.

Structure follows revenue.

90-Day Growth Plan

Month One
Secure ten to twenty small jobs
Collect testimonials

Month Two
Increase rates slightly
Create a simple one-page flyer
Reach out to property managers

Month Three
Narrow into your most profitable services
Raise rates again
Schedule recurring maintenance clients

Momentum matters more than perfection.

Startup Checklist

Basic tools
List of five services
Local posts made
Simple pricing plan
Income tracking sheet
Three testimonials

Start simple.
Improve as you go.

CHAPTER 2

House Cleaning

What This Business Really Is

House cleaning is not glamorous. It is reliable, repeatable, and in constant demand.

This business is built on trust and consistency. Clients are not hiring perfection. They are hiring relief. They want their time back.

If you are organized, dependable, and willing to work efficiently, you can begin quickly.

Why It Works

Every community has:

Dual-income households
Busy parents
Elderly homeowners
Rental properties

Cleaning is recurring. That means predictable income.

Unlike many businesses, this one creates built-in repeat customers.

How to Make Your First Dollar

Keep it simple.

Offer one service first: a standard cleaning.

Post locally:

"Residential cleaning available. Reliable, thorough, and affordable. Message for details."

Offer a discounted first clean in exchange for a testimonial.

Your goal is to secure one recurring client.

One weekly client creates momentum.

The First 30 Days

Focus on:

Securing 2–4 recurring clients
Creating a simple checklist
Tracking time spent per home
Collecting testimonials

Do not overinvest in branding.

Consistency and referrals build this business.

Supplemental vs Full-Time Path

Supplemental Model
1–3 homes per week
$800–$2,000 per month possible

Full-Time Model
5–8 homes per week
Add deep-clean services
$4,000–$6,000+ per month depending on rates

Recurring clients create stability.

When to Handle Legal and Structure

Start as a sole proprietor.

As income stabilizes:

Open separate account
Track expenses
Consider liability insurance

Check local requirements as you grow.

90-Day Growth Plan

Month One
Secure 2 recurring clients

Month Two
Raise rates slightly for new clients
Ask for referrals

Month Three
Add deep clean or move-out services

Consistency compounds.

Startup Checklist

Cleaning supplies
Simple pricing model
Local posts made
Client checklist
Income tracking sheet
2 testimonials

Start steady.
Deliver quality.

CHAPTER 3

Lawn Care

What This Business Really Is

Lawn care is a seasonal but dependable service business.

Homeowners want clean, maintained yards. Many do not want to do the work themselves.

This business rewards reliability more than skill complexity.

Why It Works

Grass grows every week.

That means recurring service opportunities.

Unlike one-time gigs, mowing can become predictable weekly income.

How to Make Your First Dollar

Start small.

Offer mowing and basic edging.

Knock on 10 doors in your neighborhood:
"I'm offering reliable weekly lawn service this season."

Post locally online.

Price simply per yard size.

Secure one recurring yard first.

The First 30 Days

Focus on:

Building 5 recurring clients
Learning time efficiency
Improving route planning

Avoid buying expensive equipment until revenue supports it.

Supplemental vs Full-Time Path

Supplemental
5 lawns per week
$1,000–$2,000 per month possible

Full-Time
20+ lawns per week
Add fertilizing, trimming, seasonal cleanup
$4,000–$8,000+ monthly in active season

Recurring contracts build predictability.

When to Handle Legal and Structure

Begin as sole proprietor.

As revenue increases:

Separate bank account
Check local permit requirements
Consider insurance

Structure grows with income.

90-Day Growth Plan

Month One
Secure 5 clients

Month Two
Optimize schedule
Raise rates for new clients

Month Three
Add upsell services

Efficiency increases profit.

Startup Checklist

Mower and trimmer
Pricing sheet
Client list
Route plan
Income tracker

Show up on schedule.
Reliability builds reputation.

CHAPTER 4

Mobile Car Detailing

What This Business Really Is

Mobile car detailing is a service business built around convenience.

Customers want their vehicles cleaned without driving to a shop.

You bring the service to them.

Why It Works

Car owners value convenience.

Busy professionals will pay for someone to clean their vehicle at home or work.

This business can start with minimal equipment and scale gradually.

How to Make Your First Dollar

Offer one service: basic interior and exterior clean.

Post locally:
"Mobile car detailing — I come to you."

Offer introductory pricing for first 5 clients.

Ask for before-and-after photos and testimonials.

The First 30 Days

Focus on:

Building 5 repeat clients
Improving speed
Learning pricing based on vehicle size

Do not overcomplicate services early.

Deliver strong results.

Supplemental vs Full-Time Path

Supplemental
2–4 cars per weekend
$1,000–$2,500 per month possible

Full-Time
3–5 vehicles per day

Add premium detailing packages
$4,000–$9,000+ per month depending on region

Skill improves margins.

When to Handle Legal and Structure

Begin as sole proprietor.

As revenue grows:

Separate bank account
Review local business requirements
Consider liability insurance

Scale responsibly.

90-Day Growth Plan

Month One
Secure 5 clients
Collect before/after photos

Month Two
Increase pricing
Offer maintenance plans

Month Three
Target corporate parking lots

Consistency builds referrals.

CHAPTER 5

Pet Sitting and Dog Walking

What This Business Really Is

Pet sitting and dog walking is a trust-based service business. You are caring for something people love. Reliability and responsibility matter more than complexity.

This business is built on consistency, communication, and showing up.

Why It Works

Pet owners travel.
Busy professionals work long hours.
Elderly owners need help.

Pets require daily care. That creates recurring demand.

How to Make Your First Dollar

Offer one simple service first: daily dog walking.

Post locally:
"Reliable dog walking and pet sitting available. References upon request."

Reach out to friends and neighbors with pets.

Offer your first week at a slightly reduced rate in exchange for a testimonial.

Secure one recurring client.

The First 30 Days

Focus on:

Building 3–5 regular clients
Creating a simple schedule
Tracking mileage and time

Keep services simple early on.

Supplemental vs Full-Time Path

Supplemental
5–10 walks per week
$500–$1,500 per month possible

Full-Time
Multiple daily walks + vacation sitting
Add overnight care
$3,000–$6,000+ per month depending on volume

Trust builds repeat bookings.

When to Handle Legal and Structure

Start as sole proprietor.

As bookings increase:

Separate business account
Consider liability insurance
Check local licensing requirements

Structure follows revenue.

90-Day Growth Plan

Month One
Secure 3 recurring clients

Month Two
Collect testimonials
Increase rates for new clients

Month Three
Add vacation packages

Reputation drives growth.

Startup Checklist

Reliable transportation
Simple pricing plan
Client schedule
Emergency contact forms
Income tracker

Be dependable.
Dependability becomes your marketing.

CHAPTER 6

Furniture Flipping

What This Business Really Is

Furniture flipping is buying undervalued items, improving them, and reselling at a profit.

This is a margin business. Your skill is in buying well and improving efficiently.

Why It Works

People frequently discard quality furniture.

Many buyers prefer refinished pieces at lower prices than retail.

There is constant supply and steady demand.

How to Make Your First Dollar

Start small.

Look for one solid wood piece priced low.

Clean, sand, repaint, or refinish simply.

Relist for a reasonable markup.

Your first goal is one profitable flip.

The First 30 Days

Focus on:

Completing 2–4 flips
Learning what sells quickly
Improving your pricing judgment

Do not overcomplicate designs.

Profit comes from efficiency.

Supplemental vs Full-Time Path

Supplemental
2–6 flips per month
$500–$2,000 possible

Full-Time
Consistent sourcing
Garage or storage workspace
$3,000–$7,000+ per month depending on volume

Margins matter more than volume.

When to Handle Legal and Structure

Begin as sole proprietor.

As inventory grows:

Track cost of goods
Separate bank account
Review resale requirements locally

Scale responsibly.

90-Day Growth Plan

Month One
Complete 2 flips

Month Two
Refine sourcing strategy

Month Three
Increase pricing confidence

Consistency improves buying instincts.

Startup Checklist

Basic tools
Transportation access
Marketplace accounts

Expense tracker
Before/after photos

Buy smart. Improve efficiently.

CHAPTER 7

Home-Based Baking Business

What This Business Really Is

A home-based baking business focuses on small-batch, specialty products rather than large-scale production.

It relies on quality, niche focus, and word-of-mouth.

Why It Works

People buy for events, gifts, and convenience.

Specialty products command premium pricing.

Local relationships create repeat customers.

How to Make Your First Dollar

Start with one specialty item.

Offer pre-orders for a specific date.

Promote locally through social media.

Secure small batch orders first.

The First 30 Days

Focus on:

Perfecting 1–2 items
Tracking ingredient costs
Gathering feedback

Avoid expanding menu too quickly.

Supplemental vs Full-Time Path

Supplemental
Weekend orders
$500–$1,500 per month possible

Full-Time
Event orders + regular clients
Wholesale relationships
$3,000–$6,000+ per month

Efficiency and pricing control profitability.

When to Handle Legal and Structure

Food laws vary by location.

Before selling regularly:

Review cottage food laws
Check labeling requirements
Understand local regulations

Operate responsibly and legally.

90-Day Growth Plan

Month One
Secure first 5 customers

Month Two
Increase pricing gradually

Month Three
Expand offerings slightly

Controlled growth reduces risk.

Startup Checklist

Approved kitchen setup
Cost tracking sheet
Simple menu

Order form
Ingredient inventory

Quality builds repeat orders.

CHAPTER 8

Handmade Product Business

What This Business Really Is

This includes soap, candles, crafts, and other small-batch products made at home.

It is product-based and brand-driven.

Why It Works

People value handmade and local products.

Small niche audiences are loyal.

Margins improve with production efficiency.

How to Make Your First Dollar

Choose one product only.

Produce a small test batch.

Offer to friends, local markets, or online marketplace.

Focus on selling out your first batch.

The First 30 Days

Focus on:

Testing demand
Tracking material costs
Improving packaging

Avoid expanding product lines too quickly.

Supplemental vs Full-Time Path

Supplemental
Small batch production
$500–$1,500 monthly possible

Full-Time
Regular production schedule
Wholesale partnerships
$3,000–$6,000+ depending on demand

Brand identity matters.

When to Handle Legal and Structure

Begin as sole proprietor.

As production grows:

Review labeling requirements
Check product safety standards
Separate bank account

Structure grows with revenue.

90-Day Growth Plan

Month One
Sell first batch

Month Two
Adjust pricing

Month Three
Expand distribution channels

Reinvest profits carefully.

Startup Checklist

Basic materials
Cost tracking sheet
Small batch production plan

Pricing model
Income tracker

Start narrow.
Improve steadily.

CHAPTER 9

Virtual Assistant

What This Business Really Is

A virtual assistant provides administrative support to business owners remotely. This can include email management, scheduling, customer communication, data entry, and light research.

You are not building a tech company. You are solving small operational problems.

Why It Works

Small businesses are overwhelmed.

Many owners cannot afford full-time staff but need part-time help.

Remote support is now normal and widely accepted.

How to Make Your First Dollar

Choose 2–3 services:
Email organization
Appointment scheduling
Customer follow-up

Message 10 small business owners per day: "I help small businesses stay organized and manage routine tasks. Would you like a few hours of support weekly?"

Offer a small trial package.

Secure one client for 5 hours per week.

The First 30 Days

Focus on:

Delivering reliability
Improving speed
Clarifying task boundaries

Do not try to offer everything.

Be excellent at a few tasks.

Supplemental vs Full-Time Path

Supplemental
5–10 hours per week
$500–$1,500 per month possible

Full-Time
25–40 billable hours weekly
$3,000–$6,000+ per month depending on rates

Specialization increases rates.

When to Handle Legal and Structure

Begin as sole proprietor. as income grows:

Separate bank account
Track invoices carefully
Understand tax obligations

Professional structure follows steady revenue.

90-Day Growth Plan

Month   One:
Secure first client

Month   Two:
Raise rates for new clients

Month Three:
Add second recurring client

Consistency builds income stability.

Startup Checklist

List of services
Simple hourly rate
Outreach message template
Invoice template
Income tracker

Start narrow. Expand later.

CHAPTER 10

Bookkeeping

What This Business Really Is

Bookkeeping is tracking income and expenses for small businesses. It is organizational work, not accounting strategy.

You are helping business owners stay clear and compliant.

Why It Works

Many small business owners dislike financial tracking.

Bookkeeping is recurring monthly work.

Clients value accuracy and reliability.

How to Make Your First Dollar

Offer basic monthly bookkeeping for small service businesses.

Contact 10 local businesses:
"I help small businesses stay organized with monthly bookkeeping support."

Offer a starter rate for your first client.

The First 30 Days

Focus on:

Understanding client systems
Tracking transactions accurately
Communicating clearly

Accuracy builds trust.

Supplemental vs Full-Time Path

Supplemental
1–3 clients
$500–$2,000 monthly possible

Full-Time
8–15 clients
$4,000–$8,000+ monthly depending on rates

Recurring contracts create predictable income.

When to Handle Legal and Structure

Begin as sole proprietor.

Understand that financial services may have local requirements.

Consult local regulations as business grows.

90-Day Growth Plan

Month One
Secure first client

Month Two
Refine workflow

Month Three
Add second client

Build slowly and accurately.

Startup Checklist

Basic accounting software knowledge
Client outreach list
Monthly reporting template
Income tracker

Precision matters.

CHAPTER 11

Social Media Management

What This Business Really Is

You manage online content for small businesses. This includes posting, responding to comments, and basic content planning.

You are helping businesses stay visible.

Why It Works

Many small businesses lack time or skill for consistent posting.

Visibility drives customer attention.

Consistency is more valuable than creativity.

How to Make Your First Dollar

Choose one platform.

Offer to manage posts for one small business for a trial month.

Reach out directly. Secure one small monthly contract.

The First 30 Days

Focus on:

Posting consistently
Tracking engagement
Improving clarity

Avoid overcomplicating strategy.

Supplemental vs Full-Time Path

Supplemental
1–3 clients
$500–$2,000 per month

Full-Time
5–10 clients
$3,000–$7,000+ monthly

Systems improve efficiency.

When to Handle Legal and Structure

Start simple.

Separate bank account once income stabilizes.

Follow platform and advertising regulations.

90-Day Growth Plan

Month One
Secure one client

Month Two
Add second client

Month Three
Raise rates

Experience increases value.

Startup Checklist

Service outline
Monthly content calendar
Basic contract template
Invoice system
Income tracker

Consistency wins.

CHAPTER 12

Graphic Design

What This Business Really Is

Graphic design solves visual communication problems for businesses.

Logos, social posts, flyers, and branding assets.

Skill and clarity matter more than equipment.

Why It Works

Every business needs visual identity.

Small businesses need affordable options.

Projects can be one-time or recurring.

How to Make Your First Dollar

Offer one clear service: logo package or social graphics.

Contact local businesses.

Offer discounted first project for testimonial.

Secure one project.

The First 30 Days

Focus on:

Delivering quality
Collecting testimonials
Refining workflow

Avoid underpricing long-term.

Supplemental vs Full-Time Path

Supplemental
Project-based income
$500–$2,000 monthly

Full-Time
Multiple recurring clients
$4,000–$8,000+ monthly

Portfolio builds pricing power.

When to Handle Legal and Structure

Begin as sole proprietor.

Use written agreements.

Separate finances once revenue stabilizes.

90-Day Growth Plan

Month One
Complete 2 projects

Month Two
Raise pricing

Month Three
Add recurring clients

Professional presentation increases value.

Startup Checklist

Portfolio samples
Service package outline
Contract template
Invoice system
Income tracker

Deliver clarity, not just creativity.

CHAPTER 13

Coaching

What This Business Really Is

Coaching helps individuals improve performance in a specific area — career, health, business, or personal development.

It is structured guidance, not therapy.

Why It Works

People seek clarity and accountability.

Specialized guidance saves time.

Trust and credibility drive income.

How to Make Your First Dollar

Define one niche clearly.

Offer free consultation calls.

Secure one paying client.

Start with short packages.

The First 30 Days

Focus on:

Delivering measurable outcomes
Collecting testimonials
Refining offer

Avoid broad positioning.

Supplemental vs Full-Time Path

Supplemental
2–5 clients
$1,000–$3,000 monthly

Full-Time
10+ clients
$5,000–$10,000+ monthly depending on pricing

Clarity increases value.

When to Handle Legal and Structure

Begin as sole proprietor.

Use written agreements.

Separate finances when income stabilizes.

90-Day Growth Plan

Month One
Secure first client

Month Two
Refine niche

Month Three
Increase pricing

Confidence builds authority.

Startup Checklist

Clear niche
Coaching outline
Session structure
Payment system
Income tracker

Specialization builds credibility.

Next we continue with:

- Resume Writing
- Online Tutoring

CHAPTER 14

Resume Writing

What This Business Really Is

Resume writing helps individuals present their experience clearly and professionally. You are not inventing skills. You are organizing and improving how they are communicated.

Clarity and structure create value.

Why It Works

Job seekers often struggle to describe their strengths.

Many are willing to pay for help that improves their chances of getting interviews.

Hiring cycles continue regardless of economic shifts.

How to Make Your First Dollar

Offer one clear service: resume rewrite.

Post in local groups:
"Professional resume writing and formatting available."

Reach out to recent graduates or job seekers.

Secure one client and deliver strong results.

The First 30 Days

Focus on:

Completing 3–5 resumes
Improving formatting templates
Collecting testimonials

Keep services simple at first.

Supplemental vs Full-Time Path

Supplemental
2–6 resumes per month
$500–$2,000 monthly possible

Full-Time
15+ resumes monthly
Add LinkedIn optimization
$3,000–$6,000+ monthly

Speed and clarity improve margins.

When to Handle Legal and Structure

Start as sole proprietor.

Use simple written agreements.

Separate finances once income stabilizes.

90-Day Growth Plan

Month One
Complete first 3 resumes

Month Two
Raise rates slightly

Month Three
Add interview coaching option

Refinement increases confidence.

Startup Checklist

Resume template
Client intake form
Pricing sheet
Payment method
Income tracker

Clarity sells.

CHAPTER 15

Online Tutoring

What This Business Really Is

Online tutoring provides subject-specific instruction remotely. You help students improve understanding and performance.

This is structured teaching, not casual help.

Why It Works

Students need support in math, language, science, and test prep.

Parents pay for measurable improvement.

Remote learning is widely accepted.

How to Make Your First Dollar

Choose one subject you know well.

Offer trial sessions at reduced rate.

Post in parent groups or education forums.

Secure one weekly student.

The First 30 Days

Focus on:

Consistent lesson structure
Tracking student progress
Collecting testimonials

Do not expand subjects too quickly.

Supplemental vs Full-Time Path

Supplemental
3–5 sessions weekly
$800–$2,000 monthly possible

Full-Time
20+ sessions weekly
$3,000–$6,000+ monthly

Specialization increases pricing power.

When to Handle Legal and Structure

Start as sole proprietor.

Separate income and expenses once steady.

Understand any educational platform requirements.

90-Day Growth Plan

Month One
Secure first recurring student

Month Two
Add second student

Month Three
Increase rates for new clients

Progress builds reputation.

Startup Checklist

Subject outline
Session structure
Scheduling system
Payment method
Income tracker

Consistency builds trust.

CHAPTER 16

Proofreading

What This Business Really Is

Proofreading corrects grammar, punctuation, and clarity errors in written material.

It is detail-focused and precision-driven work.

Why It Works

Students, authors, and businesses all produce written content.

Clear writing improves credibility.

Demand remains steady.

How to Make Your First Dollar

Offer proofreading for essays or small business materials.

Post in student groups or freelancer forums.

Secure one small project.

The First 30 Days

Focus on:

Completing small projects
Improving speed
Collecting testimonials

Avoid underpricing long-term.

Supplemental vs Full-Time Path

Supplemental
5–10 small projects monthly
$500–$1,500 possible

Full-Time
Large or recurring clients
$3,000–$6,000+ monthly

Accuracy drives referrals.

When to Handle Legal and Structure

Begin as sole proprietor.

Use simple written agreements.

Track all income.

90-Day Growth Plan

Month One
Complete 3 projects

Month Two
Raise rates

Month Three
Secure recurring client

Precision builds confidence.

Startup Checklist

Editing software
Service outline
Pricing sheet
Payment system
Income tracker

Quality earns repeat work.

CHAPTER 17

Translation Services

What This Business Really Is

Translation services convert written or spoken content from one language to another.

Accuracy and cultural understanding are essential.

Why It Works

Global communication continues to grow.

Businesses need clear multilingual communication.

Specialized translation increases value.

How to Make Your First Dollar

Offer translation in one focused niche.

Contact small businesses serving multilingual customers.

Secure one small project.

The First 30 Days

Focus on:

Building accuracy
Clarifying turnaround times
Collecting testimonials

Avoid broad specialization early.

Supplemental vs Full-Time Path

Supplemental
Small projects
$500–$1,500 monthly

Full-Time
Corporate or agency contracts
$3,000–$7,000+ monthly

Specialization increases rates.

When to Handle Legal and Structure

Start as sole proprietor.

Separate finances as income grows.

Understand confidentiality expectations.

90-Day Growth Plan

Month One
Complete 2 projects

Month Two
Increase pricing

Month Three
Target business contracts

Reputation builds stability.

Startup Checklist

Language proficiency
Service outline
Pricing sheet
Contract template
Income tracker

Accuracy builds trust.

CHAPTER 18

Voiceover Work

What This Business Really Is

Voiceover work provides narration for advertisements, videos, audiobooks, and training materials.

Clarity and tone matter more than equipment early on.

Why It Works

Businesses and creators constantly need audio content.

Remote recording is standard.

Small projects lead to recurring work.

How to Make Your First Dollar

Create a short demo recording.

Offer narration for short videos.

Contact small content creators.

Secure one paid project.

The First 30 Days

Focus on:

Improving recording quality
Completing small projects
Building portfolio

Avoid investing heavily in equipment early.

Supplemental vs Full-Time Path

Supplemental
Small projects
$500–$1,500 monthly

Full-Time
Recurring contracts
$3,000–$8,000+ monthly

Skill and consistency raise rates.

When to Handle Legal and Structure

Start as sole proprietor.

Use clear usage agreements.

Separate income once consistent.

90-Day Growth Plan

Month One
Complete first 3 projects

Month Two
Raise rates

Month Three
Secure repeat client

Quality drives referrals.

Startup Checklist

Basic microphone
Quiet recording space
Demo sample
Pricing sheet
Income tracker

Deliver clarity and professionalism.

CHAPTER 19

Blogging

What This Business Really Is

Blogging is building a content asset around a specific topic. It is not random writing. It is structured publishing that attracts a defined audience.

Income comes later — from traffic, trust, and consistency.

Why It Works

People search online daily for information.

Well-written, focused content continues working long after it is published.

Over time, content becomes an asset.

How to Make Your First Dollar

Choose one focused niche:
Home improvement
Budget cooking
Fitness over 40
Local travel

Create 5 useful articles.

Add simple affiliate links or basic ads.

Your first goal is not high income. It is proof of concept.

The First 30 Days

Focus on:

Publishing consistently
Improving clarity
Learning basic keyword research

Avoid obsessing over design.

Content matters more than appearance.

Supplemental vs Full-Time Path

Supplemental
Slow growth
$100–$1,000 monthly after traction

Full-Time
High traffic niche
$3,000–$10,000+ monthly over time

This is a long-term model.

When to Handle Legal and Structure

Start simple.

As income grows:

Separate finances
Understand advertising tax rules

Structure follows revenue.

90-Day Growth Plan

Month One
Publish consistently

Month Two
Optimize content

Month Three
Add affiliate partnerships

Patience builds asset value.

Startup Checklist

Domain name
Simple website
Content plan
Affiliate account
Income tracker

Consistency wins long-term.

CHAPTER 20

Affiliate Marketing

What This Business Really Is

Affiliate marketing earns commission by recommending products or services.

You do not own the product. You connect buyers to sellers.

Trust drives income.

Why It Works

Companies reward referrals.

Consumers trust trusted recommendations.

Low startup cost makes it accessible.

How to Make Your First Dollar

Choose one product category.

Write one helpful review or tutorial.

Share through blog, social media, or email list.

Focus on clarity and honesty.

The First 30 Days

Focus on:

Understanding audience needs
Producing helpful content
Tracking clicks and conversions

Avoid chasing too many products.

Supplemental vs Full-Time Path

Supplemental
Small commissions
$100–$1,000 monthly

Full-Time
High traffic + multiple partnerships
$3,000–$10,000+ monthly

Trust compounds.

When to Handle Legal and Structure

Disclose affiliate relationships.

As revenue grows:

Separate finances
Track commission income carefully

Operate transparently.

90-Day Growth Plan

Month One
Publish first reviews

Month Two
Improve content

Month Three
Expand into related products

Authority increases income.

Startup Checklist

Affiliate account
Disclosure statement
Content plan
Tracking sheet
Income tracker

Honesty builds sustainability.

CHAPTER 21

Digital Products

What This Business Really Is

Digital products include templates, guides, checklists, or downloadable tools.

You create once and sell repeatedly.

Why It Works

People value shortcuts and structure.

Digital delivery removes inventory costs.

Margins are high after creation.

How to Make Your First Dollar

Identify one common problem.

Create a simple solution:
Budget spreadsheet

Meal plan template
Business checklist

Sell through a simple platform.

Your goal is one sale.

The First 30 Days

Focus on:

Refining the product
Gathering feedback
Improving clarity

Avoid creating too many products early.

Supplemental vs Full-Time Path

Supplemental
Occasional sales
$200–$1,000 monthly

Full-Time
Multiple products
Email list growth
$3,000–$8,000+ monthly

Leverage increases with scale.

When to Handle Legal and Structure

Start as sole proprietor.

As sales grow:

Separate business finances
Review digital tax rules

Structure expands with revenue.

90-Day Growth Plan

Month One
Launch first product

Month Two
Improve product

Month Three
Add second product

Reinvestment fuels growth.

Startup Checklist

Product idea
Creation tool
Sales platform
Pricing model
Income tracker

Solve one problem well.

CHAPTER 22

Online Course Creation

What This Business Really Is

Online courses package structured knowledge into lessons.

You are teaching a defined skill or outcome.

Why It Works

People pay for structured learning.

Courses save time and reduce confusion.

Once created, they can sell repeatedly.

How to Make Your First Dollar

Choose one focused topic.

Outline 5–10 short lessons.

Record with simple equipment.

Pre-sell before full production if possible.

Secure first enrollment.

The First 30 Days

Focus on:

Clear outcomes
Simple lesson structure
Gathering feedback

Avoid perfectionism.

Supplemental vs Full-Time Path

Supplemental
Small cohort
$500–$2,000 monthly

Full-Time
Multiple launches
Membership model
$5,000–$15,000+ monthly

Authority builds leverage.

When to Handle Legal and Structure

Begin simply.

As revenue grows:

Separate finances
Understand platform policies

Protect intellectual property when scaling.

90-Day Growth Plan

Month One
Outline and pre-sell

Month Two
Launch first version

Month Three
Improve and relaunch

Improvement builds reputation.

Startup Checklist

Course outline
Recording tool
Sales platform
Payment system
Income tracker

Teach clearly. Improve consistently.

CHAPTER 23

Pressure Washing Services

What This Business Really Is

Pressure washing is a high-impact, visible transformation service. You are restoring surfaces — driveways, sidewalks, siding, decks, fences — back to a cleaner, brighter state.

This is not construction work. It is restoration.

The value is visual. Customers see immediate results.

That visual difference justifies pricing.

Why It Works

Most homeowners do not own commercial-grade pressure washers.

Even those who do often underestimate the time and effort required.

Algae, mold, dirt buildup, and weather staining accumulate gradually. Many homeowners delay cleaning until the property begins to look neglected.

Pressure washing offers:

- Immediate improvement
- Relatively low material cost
- High perceived value
- Strong word-of-mouth potential

It is especially strong in suburban neighborhoods.

How to Make Your First Dollar

You do not need a truck-mounted commercial system to begin.

Start small.

Offer driveway or sidewalk cleaning only.

Walk your neighborhood and look for visible buildup.

Knock and say:

"I'm offering driveway and sidewalk cleaning in the area this week. I noticed some buildup that can be removed quickly. Would you like a free estimate?"

Price simply by square footage or flat driveway rate.

Your goal is not branding.

Your goal is one paid job and before-and-after photos.

Equipment to Start

You can begin with:

- A reliable pressure washer
- Surface cleaner attachment
- Extension hose
- Basic safety gear

Do not overspend at the beginning.

Let revenue fund upgrades.

The First 30 Days

Focus on:

Completing 5–10 small jobs
Taking clear before-and-after photos
Asking every client for a referral
Posting your results locally

Results sell this business.

Supplemental vs Full-Time Path

Supplemental
Weekends only

5–10 jobs monthly
$1,000–$3,000 possible depending on pricing

Full-Time
Daily scheduling
Add house washing, deck cleaning, fence restoration
$4,000–$10,000+ monthly depending on region

Upsells increase income without adding many new customers.

Pricing Strategy

Do not race to the bottom.

Price based on:

Time required
Equipment wear
Water usage
Fuel
Skill

Underpricing creates burnout.

When to Handle Legal and Structure

Start as sole proprietor.

As volume increases:

Open separate bank account
Consider liability insurance
Check local water regulations

Operate professionally.

90-Day Growth Plan

Month One
Secure 5 jobs
Build photo portfolio

Month Two
Increase pricing slightly
Offer bundled services

Month Three
Target property managers
Offer seasonal maintenance

Momentum compounds quickly in visual businesses.

Startup Checklist

Pressure washer
Basic attachments
Safety equipment
Pricing sheet

Before-and-after photo folder
Income tracker

Deliver visible results.
Let transformation market your work.

CHAPTER 24

Junk Removal

What This Business Really Is

Junk removal is the organized removal of unwanted items from homes, garages, basements, and properties.

It is a labor business with strong margins when managed properly.

You are solving clutter problems.

Why It Works

People accumulate items faster than they remove them.

Moving, downsizing, remodeling, and estate cleanouts create demand.

Many people lack trucks or the physical ability to haul large items.

Convenience drives payment.

How to Make Your First Dollar

Start small.

Offer garage cleanouts or single-item removal.

Post locally:

"Affordable junk removal and haul-away services. Fast response."

Price based on:

Truck space used
Time required
Disposal fees

Secure one small job.

Managing Costs

Profit comes from margin control.

Know:

Landfill fees
Fuel cost
Time invested

Whenever possible, resell usable items or donate them.

Efficiency increases income.

The First 30 Days

Focus on:

Completing 3–5 jobs
Understanding disposal logistics
Building referral relationships

Take photos for proof of work.

Supplemental vs Full-Time Path

Supplemental
2–4 jobs weekly
$1,000–$3,000 monthly

Full-Time
Daily scheduling
Larger cleanouts
$5,000 $12,000 ｜ monthly depending on volume

This business scales with labor help.

Scaling Strategy

After consistent demand:

Hire part-time labor
Increase truck capacity
Partner with realtors

Systemization increases volume.

When to Handle Legal and Structure

Begin as sole proprietor.

As jobs increase:

Separate bank account
Check waste disposal regulations
Consider liability insurance

Operate cleanly and responsibly.

90-Day Growth Plan

Month One
Complete first 5 jobs

Month Two
Increase pricing
Improve route efficiency

Month Three
Target estate cleanouts
Develop referral partnerships

Controlled growth builds stability.

Startup Checklist

Truck or trailer
Basic labor tools
Gloves and safety gear
Disposal plan
Pricing structure
Income tracker

Remove clutter.
Deliver relief.

CHAPTER 25

Local Moving and Labor Services

What This Business Really Is

Local moving and labor services focus on small apartment moves, furniture rearranging, and loading or unloading trucks.

You are selling strength, reliability, and efficiency.

Why It Works

People move frequently.

Not everyone can lift heavy items.

Many renters need short-distance help.

It is straightforward, physical work.

How to Make Your First Dollar

Offer labor-only moving assistance.

Post: "Reliable moving labor available for small moves, loading, unloading, and furniture relocation."

Partner with truck rental customers.

Secure one small move.

The First 30 Days

Focus on:

Completing 3–5 moves
Learning time estimates
Improving efficiency

Ask for referrals immediately after job completion.

Supplemental vs Full-Time Path

Supplemental
Weekend moves
$1,000–$2,500 monthly

Full-Time
Multiple weekly bookings
Team-based model
$5,000–$12,000+ monthly

Scaling requires helpers.

Risk Management

This is physical work.

Protect yourself:

Lift properly
Use equipment
Carry insurance as you scale

Professionalism builds trust.

When to Handle Legal and Structure

Begin as sole proprietor.

As revenue stabilizes:

Separate finances
Consider insurance
Understand local transport regulations

Scale carefully.

90-Day Growth Plan

Month One
Secure first 3 jobs

Month Two
Increase pricing
Add basic equipment

Month Three
Recruit part-time help

Efficiency multiplies income.

Startup Checklist

Basic moving equipment
Reliable transportation
Clear pricing sheet
Service agreement
Income tracker

Strength and reliability build reputation.

CHAPTER 26

Case Study: Handyman

Building a $3,500/Month Handyman Business in 90 Days

This is not a fantasy scenario.

This is what realistic progress looks like when someone commits to one model and executes consistently.

Starting Point

Mark is 42 years old.

Full-time warehouse employee.
No business experience.
Basic tools in his garage.
$800 in savings.

He is not trying to quit his job immediately.

He wants $2,000 extra per month.

That is his target.

Week 1: The Decision Phase

Mark does not build a website.

He does not form an LLC.

He writes down five services he knows he can perform confidently:

- Replace light fixtures
- Install ceiling fans
- Repair drywall holes
- Replace faucets
- Install shelves

He posts in three local Facebook groups.

He texts 15 people he knows.

He gets two responses.

One job books.

$175 to replace two light fixtures.

It takes him 2.5 hours.

His confidence increases.

Week 2–3: Early Friction

He completes four small jobs.

Total revenue: $820.

Mistakes:

- Underpriced two jobs
- Took too long on drywall repair
- Forgot to track mileage

He feels doubt.

He considers raising prices but fears losing clients.

Instead, he focuses on speed.

He watches two drywall repair tutorials.

Improves technique.

Week 4: Momentum Begins

He completes 8 total jobs.

Revenue for Month 1: $1,650.

He realizes something important:

People are not paying for perfection.
They are paying for reliability.

He shows up on time.
He communicates clearly.
He cleans up after himself.

That alone differentiates him.

Month 2: Refinement

Mark adjusts pricing by 15% for new customers.

He creates a simple one-page flyer.

He reaches out to two property managers.

One responds.

Now he has recurring small repair requests.

Month 2 revenue: $2,900.

He is working evenings and Saturdays.

He is tired — but motivated.

Month 3: Stabilization

He identifies his most profitable services:

- Fixture replacement
- Fan installation
- Minor plumbing

He stops advertising drywall repairs.

Too time-consuming.

He increases rates again for new customers.

Month 3 revenue: $3,540.

He now understands:

Income follows focus.

What Made the Difference

Not equipment.

Not branding.

Not perfect planning.

Three things:

1. He committed for 90 days.
2. He tracked numbers.
3. He improved something each week.

What He Would Do Differently

- Raise prices sooner
- Track expenses from day one
- Say no to low-margin jobs earlier

Clarity came through action.

Where He Goes Next

He now has options:

Remain supplemental
Reduce warehouse hours
Or expand into full-time

The key point:

He did not leap.

He built.

This is what 90 days of focused execution can produce in a practical service business.

CHAPTER 27

Case Study: Cleaning

Turning a Cleaning Side Job Into $6,000 per Month

This is what steady expansion looks like when someone treats a small service like a business instead of
a chore.

Starting Point

Angela is 36.

She works part-time at a medical office.
Two children.
Limited savings.
No business background.

She starts cleaning because a friend asks for help before
hosting guests.

She earns $120 for four hours.

She realizes something important:

She made more in four hours than she does in an eight-hour shift.

That observation changes her thinking.

Month 1: Testing the Idea

Angela decides to try cleaning seriously for 30 days.

She creates a simple offer:

Standard residential cleaning
Flat rate based on home size

She posts in two local groups.

She books three homes.

Month 1 revenue: $1,280.

Problems she encounters:

- Underestimated time required
- Underpriced deep cleans
- Brought too many supplies

She feels physically tired.

But she also feels encouraged.

Month 2: Systemizing

Angela stops treating each house differently.

She builds a checklist:

Kitchen
Bathrooms
Floors
Dusting
Surfaces

She times herself.

She reduces cleaning time per home by 45 minutes simply by working in sequence.

She raises rates for new clients by 20%.

She introduces a recurring discount:

Weekly and bi-weekly clients receive priority scheduling.

Month 2 revenue: $3,400.

Now she sees predictability forming.

Month 3: Stabilization

Angela identifies something critical.

Deep cleans pay more — but take too long.

Recurring weekly clients produce steadier income.

She shifts focus.

She prioritizes:

Small to mid-size homes
Bi-weekly service
Predictable scheduling

She drops one difficult client.

Raises rates again for new clients.

Month 3 revenue: $6,050.

She now works:

Four days per week
Six hours per day

Her part-time job becomes optional.

What Made the Difference

Not better mops.

Not branding.

Three factors:

1. She standardized her process.
2. She prioritized recurring income.

3. She raised prices gradually instead of staying underpriced.

Consistency created stability.

Mistakes She Would Avoid Next Time

- Starting too low on pricing
- Saying yes to every client
- Accepting irregular scheduling

Structure matters.

Where She Goes Next

Angela has options:

Remain solo.
Hire one part-time helper.
Add deep-clean premium packages seasonally.

The business did not explode overnight. It stabilized through repetition.

The lesson: Service businesses become powerful when they become predictable.

Now the third case

CHAPTER 28

Case Study

Growing a Virtual Assistant

Parttime Into Full-Time Income

This example shows how skill-based businesses scale differently from physical labor businesses.

Starting Point

Daniel is 29.

Full-time customer service representative.
Comfortable with email, scheduling, spreadsheets.
No formal business training.

He wants remote flexibility.

He chooses virtual assistance.

Month 1: Outreach and Rejection

Daniel commits to messaging 10 small business owners per day.

Most ignore him.

Some decline politely.

One responds.

He secures a trial:

5 hours per week
$25 per hour

Month 1 revenue: $500.

He feels discouraged — but continues.

Month 2: Refinement

Daniel notices he is spending too much time on low-value tasks.

He narrows his offer to:

Inbox management
Customer response
Calendar organization

He improves efficiency.

He increases rate to $30/hour for new prospects.

He secures second client.

Month 2 revenue: $1,800.

Momentum builds.

Month 3: Positioning Shift

Daniel realizes something powerful.

Clients do not want a "virtual assistant."

They want problems solved.

He repositions his message:

"I help small businesses reduce customer response time and improve organization."

This subtle shift increases response rate.

He increases rate to $35/hour.

Secures third client.

Month 3 revenue: $3,750.

Month 4–6: Full-Time Transition

He gradually increases hours.

Adds retainer packages instead of hourly billing.

Moves to flat monthly agreements.

Month 6 revenue: $6,200.

He resigns from his job.

What Made the Difference

Not certifications.

Not a website.

Three factors:

1. Consistent daily outreach.
2. Narrowing his offer.
3. Repositioning around outcomes instead of tasks.

What He Would Do Differently

- Specialize sooner
- Avoid underpricing at the start
- Track time more carefully

Clarity came through iteration.

Key Takeaway

Skill-based businesses scale through positioning.

The more clearly you define the outcome, the higher your earning potential.

CHAPTER 29

Pricing

The Skill That Determines Your Income

M ost beginners do not fail because of effort.
They fail because of pricing.

You can work hard, stay consistent, deliver quality service — and still feel stuck financially if your pricing is wrong.

Pricing is not emotional.

It is math.

And math determines control.

Why Most Beginners Underprice

There are three common reasons:

1. Fear of rejection
2. Comparing themselves to competitors

3. Not knowing their real costs

Beginners assume lower prices will bring more customers.

Sometimes it does.

But low prices also attract:

- High-maintenance clients
- Price-sensitive customers
- Low loyalty

Underpricing creates exhaustion.

Start With Basic Income Math

Let's remove emotion and calculate clearly.

If your goal is:

$4,000 per month

And you can realistically work:

100 billable hours per month

Then your minimum average hourly revenue must be:

$40 per hour

But that is gross revenue.

Now subtract:

Supplies
Fuel
Taxes
Equipment wear
Unpaid administrative time

If those costs equal 25%, your effective hourly target becomes:

$50–$55 per hour.

This is how pricing is built.

Not by guessing.
Not by copying competitors.
By reverse engineering your goal.

Flat Rate vs Hourly Pricing

Hourly Pricing:

Pros:

- Simple to calculate
- Protects you from underestimating time

Cons:

- Caps income at time available
- Encourages slower work in some cases

Flat Rate Pricing:

Pros:

- Rewards efficiency
- Easier for clients to understand
- Higher income potential

Cons:

- Requires accurate time estimation

For service businesses, flat rate often wins — once you understand your numbers.

Calculate Your Real Hourly Rate

Example: House Cleaning

You charge $150 per home.

Time spent:
3 hours cleaning
30 minutes travel
30 minutes preparation

Total time: 4 hours.

Effective hourly rate:
$150 ÷ 4 = $37.50

If your goal is $50 per hour, this is underpriced.

This is how clarity is created.

The 20% Rule for Raising Prices

When demand is steady:

Raise rates for new customers by 10–20%.

If bookings continue without resistance, you were underpriced.

Never raise prices for existing loyal customers immediately.

Phase increases gradually.

Pricing increases should feel controlled — not desperate.

Pricing Based on Value, Not Time

Some services produce visible transformation.

Pressure washing.
Graphic design.
Deep cleaning.
Resume writing.

If a customer receives clear, measurable benefit, pricing can reflect value — not just hours worked.

Example:

If a resume rewrite helps someone secure a higher-paying job, your fee is small compared to their gain.

Value-based pricing increases margin.

Avoid Competing on Price Alone

If your only advantage is being cheaper, you will attract unstable demand.

Compete on:

Reliability
Speed
Communication
Professionalism

Price becomes one factor — not the only one.

Know Your Minimum Viable Pricing

Calculate:

Monthly income goal
÷
Realistic billable hours

Add 20–30% for overhead and taxes.

That number is your floor.

Never price below it long-term.

Temporary discounts are fine.

Permanent underpricing is not.

The Breakpoint Calculation

Ask:

At what price does this stop being worth my time?

If you would resent doing the job at that rate, it is too low.

Resentment destroys discipline.

Package Your Services

Instead of offering:

Single small services at low rates,

Bundle them.

Example:

Instead of:
Faucet replacement – $80
Shelf installation – $60

Offer:
Home Repair Package – $225

Bundling increases average job size.

Larger tickets reduce client volume pressure.

When to Say No

Not every customer is profitable.

If a client:

Negotiates aggressively
Cancels frequently
Creates excessive revisions
Consumes unpaid time

They reduce your effective hourly rate.

It is better to serve fewer profitable clients than many draining ones.

Long-Term Pricing Strategy

Year 1:
Focus on accuracy and stabilization.

Year 2:
Increase rates strategically.

Year 3:
Specialize and position for premium clients.

Pricing evolves with skill and confidence.

Final Pricing Principle

If you work constantly but feel financially stuck, pricing is the problem.

Track your time.
Track your margin.
Calculate your real hourly rate.
Adjust deliberately.

Income does not rise by accident.

It rises by design.

CHAPTER 30

Finding Customers

Without Paid Advertising

Most beginners believe customers come from advertising.

They don't.

They come from visibility and repetition.

Paid ads can work later. But in the beginning, you need:

Direct outreach
Local positioning
Referral leverage
Consistency

You do not need a marketing budget.

You need activity.

Start With Proximity

The easiest customers are closest to you.

Your neighborhood.
Your town.
Your existing network.

Start where trust is easiest to build.

Post in:

Local Facebook groups
Neighborhood apps
Community boards

Keep the message simple:

What you offer
Who it's for
How to contact you

No hype.
No exaggeration.

Clear and direct.

The 10-10-10 Rule

Every week:

Message 10 people directly
Comment on 10 local posts
Follow up with 10 previous contacts

Most people post once and wait.

Professionals follow up repeatedly.

Income follows activity.

Use Before-and-After Proof

For visual businesses:

Cleaning
Pressure washing
Handyman
Detailing

Photos close deals.

Document your work.

Post results consistently.

Proof builds credibility faster than promises.

The Referral Multiplier

After every completed job, ask:

"Do you know anyone else who could use this?"

Do not feel awkward.

If you did good work, referrals are natural.

One satisfied client can become three.

Over time, referrals reduce marketing effort.

Build Micro-Partnerships

You do not need large contracts.

You need small connections.

Examples:

Handyman → Property managers
Cleaning → Realtors
Virtual assistant → Local business owners
Lawn care → HOA contacts

Partnerships create recurring opportunity.

Script for Direct Outreach

Keep it simple.

"Hi, I'm offering [specific service] locally. I help [specific type of customer] solve [specific problem]. If you ever need help, I'd be glad to connect."

Short.
Direct.
Professional.

Most outreach fails because it is too long.

Follow-Up Is Where Sales Happen

Many prospects do not respond immediately.

That does not mean no.

Follow up one week later.

Then two weeks later.

Polite persistence builds trust.

Flyers Still Work

Physical visibility matters.

Simple flyer:
Service
Phone number
Short benefit statement

Place in:

Local bulletin boards
Community centers
Small businesses (with permission)

Offline marketing has less competition.

Offer a Limited Starter Package

Instead of selling everything at once, sell one entry offer.

Example:

Handyman: "3 small repairs for $199"
Cleaning: "First standard clean discount"
VA: "5-hour starter package"

Low-risk entry increases trial.

After trust builds, upsell.

Build a Simple Review Strategy

After job completion, send:

"Would you mind leaving a short review? It helps small businesses like mine."

Online reviews create passive marketing.

Five strong reviews can change response rates dramatically.

The Weekly Marketing Block

Schedule two hours per week dedicated only to outreach.

No multitasking.

No distractions.

Marketing is not random.

It is scheduled.

Consistency Beats Creativity

You do not need clever slogans.

You need repetition.

Post weekly.
Follow up weekly.
Ask for referrals weekly.

Marketing is not magic.

It is math.

More visibility = more conversations.
More conversations = more customers.

Final Principle

If customers are not coming in, increase activity — not anxiety.

Track:

Messages sent
Posts made

Conversations started
Follow-ups completed

When numbers rise, income follows.

Marketing is a discipline.

Treat it like one.

CHAPTER 31

Handling Slow Months

And Income Gaps

Every business — especially service-based or home-based income — experiences slow periods.

If you expect steady upward growth every month, you will become discouraged quickly.

Income fluctuates.

Professionals prepare for that.

Understand the Income Cycle

Most small businesses follow a pattern:

Launch phase – inconsistent income
Stabilization phase – moderate predictability
Growth phase – stronger months
Correction phase – temporary slowdown

Slow months are not failure.

They are part of the cycle.

The key is preparation.

Build a 30–60 Day Buffer

Once revenue becomes steady, begin setting aside reserves.

Start small.

Even $50–$100 per week builds protection.

Your goal is eventually:

One month of operating expenses saved.
Then two months.

This removes panic.

Panic leads to bad pricing and bad decisions.

Track Trends, Not Emotions

When a slow week hits, do not react emotionally.

Look at your numbers:

Are inquiries down?
Are bookings down?

Are cancellations up?
Is it seasonal?

Data creates clarity.

Emotion creates instability.

Increase Activity During Slow Periods

When revenue dips, increase outreach.

Send more messages.
Post more results.
Contact previous clients.

Slow months are often marketing gaps from previous weeks.

Fill the pipeline.

Offer Limited Promotions Strategically

Do not permanently drop pricing.

Instead, create time-bound offers.

Example:

"Spring Clean Special"
"End-of-Month Openings Available"
"Limited Scheduling Discount"

This increases urgency without damaging long-term positioning.

Add Temporary High-Cash Tasks

During slow periods, consider short-term cash injections:

One-day cleanouts
Small repair packages
Short consulting blocks
Flash product offers

These create quick cash flow without changing your core model.

Reduce Low-Margin Work

Sometimes slow months reveal inefficiencies.

Ask:

What services are draining time?
Which clients are high-maintenance?
Where is profit leaking?

Cutting weak areas strengthens the base.

Avoid Desperation Pricing

Lowering prices out of fear trains clients to wait.

Instead:

Increase visibility.
Increase outreach.
Increase follow-up.

Keep pricing stable.

Emotional Discipline

The hardest part of slow months is psychological.

Doubt increases.
Comparison increases.
Fear increases.

Remember:

Income is built over months, not days.

Track activity.
Track revenue.
Track growth over quarters.

Zoom out.

The Long-Term View

Month-to-month income may fluctuate.

Year-to-year income should rise.

If your annual revenue is increasing, you are progressing — even if some months dip.

Stability is built through preparation, not luck.

Final Principle

Slow months are tests of discipline.

Those who prepare survive them calmly.

Those who panic sabotage progress.

Plan ahead.
Save steadily.
Track consistently.

Stability is built intentionally.

Now, your final conclusion.

Replace any previous closing section with this:

CONCLUSION

The Discipline to Build

You began this book with an idea.

The idea of building something of your own.
The idea of reducing dependence.
The idea of turning effort into control.

Now you have more than ideas.

You have models.
You have systems.
You have case examples.
You have execution structure.
You have pricing clarity.
You have marketing discipline.
You have a framework for handling slow periods.

What remains is not information.

It is decision.

Most people will read books like this and feel inspired.

Few will act consistently.
Fewer will stay committed when growth feels slow.
Even fewer will track numbers and improve deliberately.

The separation is not talent.

It is discipline.

You do not need all 25 business models.

You need one.

You do not need perfect timing.

You need ninety focused days.

You do not need immediate freedom.

You need gradual control.

Control is built in layers.

One income stream.
Stabilized.

Then strengthened.

Then multiplied.

Over time, small, repeated actions compound.

Confidence grows from proof.
Proof comes from execution.
Execution requires structure.

You now have structure.

The opportunity is not rare.

The willingness to execute consistently is.

Start small.
Track everything.
Improve one thing at a time.
Reinvest intelligently.
Raise prices deliberately.
Protect your margin.
Build reserves.
Stay disciplined.

Home-based income is not about location.

It is about ownership.

Ownership of effort.
Ownership of numbers.
Ownership of direction.

When you control even part of your income, anxiety decreases.

When anxiety decreases, decisions improve.

When decisions improve, life expands.

That expansion does not come from luck. It comes from disciplined construction.

Choose one path.

Commit fully.

Build deliberately.

And do not stop at the first sign of friction. The courage to begin brought you here.

The discipline to continue will take you further.

Now build.

www.ingramcontent.com/pod-product-compliance
Lightning Source LLC
Chambersburg PA
CBHW060858170526
45158CB00001B/405